The ♥ COMP DANCE Life

Survival Guide and Keepsake Journal for Moms

scan here

Visit us at www.TheCompDanceLife.com for Dance Mom freebies!

the
COMP DANCE
Life

"Dance mom life: where coffee, hairspray, and bobby pins hold everything together."

Dates	Comp Name	Location

the
COMP DANCE
Life

"Being a dance mom is 10% making sure your kid is ready and 90% finding the missing dance shoe."

The Comp Mom, ♥
Monthly Planner

Month _____

Monday	Tuesday	Wednesday	Thursday	Friday	Saturday	Sunday

Notes

_____

_____

_____

the
COMP DANCE
Life

"You know you're a dance mom when you have glitter in places glitter shouldn't be."

The Comp Mom Monthly Planner

Month _____

Monday	Tuesday	Wednesday	Thursday	Friday	Saturday	Sunday

Notes

_____

_____

_____

the COMP DANCE Life

"You know you're a dance mom when you can rhinestone anything—even in your sleep!"

The Comp Mom Monthly Planner

Month _____

Monday	Tuesday	Wednesday	Thursday	Friday	Saturday	Sunday

Notes

_____

_____

_____

the
COMP DANCE
Life

"Who needs sleep when there's always a costume to bedazzle?"

The Comp Mom, Monthly Planner

Month _____

Monday	Tuesday	Wednesday	Thursday	Friday	Saturday	Sunday

Notes

_____

_____

_____

the COMP DANCE Life

"Dance mom rule #1: Never ask how much the costume costs. Just smile and swipe the card."

The Comp Mom ♥
Monthly Planner

Month _____

Monday	Tuesday	Wednesday	Thursday	Friday	Saturday	Sunday

Notes

_____

_____

_____

the
COMP DANCE
Life

"You know you're a dance mom when you can do a full makeup look in the car with no mirror."

The Comp Mom
Monthly Planner

Month _____

Monday	Tuesday	Wednesday	Thursday	Friday	Saturday	Sunday

Notes
_____
_____
_____

the COMP DANCE Life

"You know you're a dance mom when your car doubles as a dressing room, makeup studio, and cafeteria."

The Comp Mom Monthly Planner

Month _____

Monday	Tuesday	Wednesday	Thursday	Friday	Saturday	Sunday

Notes

_____

_____

_____

the
COMP DANCE
Life

"Being a dance mom means your purse always has at least one stray bobby pin and a tube of emergency lipstick."

The Comp Mom, Monthly Planner

Month _____

Monday	Tuesday	Wednesday	Thursday	Friday	Saturday	Sunday

Notes

_____

_____

_____

the
COMP DANCE
Life

"I may not be a professional dancer, but I could choreograph a ballet while juggling sequins and snack packs."

The Comp Mom Monthly Planner

Month _____

Monday	Tuesday	Wednesday	Thursday	Friday	Saturday	Sunday

Notes

_____

_____

_____

the
COMP DANCE
Life

"Dance mom superpower: Watching a solo, filming, and holding my breath all at the same time."

The Comp Mom Monthly Planner

Month _____

Monday	Tuesday	Wednesday	Thursday	Friday	Saturday	Sunday

Notes

_____

_____

_____

the
COMP DANCE
Life

"Other moms talk about weekend getaways.
Dance moms talk about weekend get-ready-for-the-next-competition."

The Comp Mom Monthly Planner

Month _____

Monday	Tuesday	Wednesday	Thursday	Friday	Saturday	Sunday

Notes

_____

_____

_____

the
COMP DANCE
Life

"You know you're a dance mom when you're more stressed
about the quick costume change than your dancer is."

The Comp Mom Monthly Planner

Month _____

Monday	Tuesday	Wednesday	Thursday	Friday	Saturday	Sunday

Notes

_____

_____

_____

Costume Measurements Guide

Girth

To measure the girth, start from the center of one shoulder, down through the crotch, and back up to the same shoulder, ensuring the tape measure remains snug against the body.

Bust/Chest

To measure the bust/chest, wrap a flexible tape measure around the fullest part of your chest, ensuring it's snug but not too tight, and measure while standing upright.

Waist

To measure the waist, wrap a flexible tape measure around the narrowest part of your torso, typically just above the belly button, ensuring it's snug but not too tight.

Hips

To measure the hips, wrap a flexible tape measure around the widest part of your buttocks and hips while standing upright.

Inseam

To measure an inseam, take a flexible tape measure and measure from the crotch down to the ankle along the inside of the leg.

Costume Measurements

Dancer				
Girth				
Bust/Chest				
Waist				
Hips				
Inseam				

 # Shoe Sizes

Dancer _____

Genre	Brand	Size

Shoe Sizes

Dancer _____

Genre	Brand	Size

 # Shoe Sizes

Dancer _____

Genre	Brand	Size

 # Shoe Sizes

Dancer _____

Genre	Brand	Size

the
COMP DANCE
Life

"You know you're a dance mom when you say, 'You got this!' more times in a day than you breathe."

Dance Class Schedule

Dancer

Monday	Tuesday	Wednesday	Thursday	Friday	Saturday	Sunday

Dance Class Schedule

Dancer

Monday	Tuesday	Wednesday	Thursday	Friday	Saturday	Sunday

Dance Class Schedule

Dancer

Monday	Tuesday	Wednesday	Thursday	Friday	Saturday	Sunday

the
COMP DANCE
Life

"You know you're a dance mom when your idea of 'relaxation' is sitting in a studio watching a 3-hour rehearsal."

Dance Payments

Payment $	Due Date	Paid
		☐
		☐
		☐
		☐
		☐
		☐
		☐
		☐
		☐
		☐

the COMP DANCE Life

"Being a dance mom means living on caffeine, surviving on glitter, and knowing the true definition of 'hurry up and wait!'"

Skill Goals

Dancer

Skill	Achieved
	☐
	☐
	☐
	☐
	☐
	☐
	☐
	☐
	☐
	☐
	☐
	☐

Skill Goals

Dancer

Skill	Achieved
	☐
	☐
	☐
	☐
	☐
	☐
	☐
	☐
	☐
	☐
	☐

Skill Goals

Dancer

Skill	Achieved
	☐
	☐
	☐
	☐
	☐
	☐
	☐
	☐
	☐
	☐
	☐
	☐

Skill Goals

Dancer

Skill	Achieved
	☐
	☐
	☐
	☐
	☐
	☐
	☐
	☐
	☐
	☐
	☐

Skill Goals

Dancer

Skill	Achieved
	☐
	☐
	☐
	☐
	☐
	☐
	☐
	☐
	☐
	☐
	☐
	☐

the
COMP DANCE
Life

"Behind every great dancer is a dance mom, juggling schedules,
fixing last-minute costumes, and cheering with a heart full of pride!"

Dances

Dancer	Dance	Genre	Size	Age Level

Dances

Dancer	Dance	Genre	Size	Age Level

Dances

Dancer	Dance	Genre	Size	Age Level

the
COMP DANCE
Life

"Only a dance mom can turn a car ride into a dressing room,
a snack bar, and a pep rally—all before 8 AM!"

Choreo Schedule

Dancer	Date	Dance	Time

Choreo Schedule

Dancer	Date	Dance	Time

Choreo Schedule

Dancer	Date	Dance	Time

the
COMP DANCE
Life

"Who needs a gym membership when you're a dance mom?
Lifting dance bags, hauling props, and sprinting to the
dressing room counts as cardio, right?"

Costumes

Dancer _____

Dance	Costume	Accessories	Shoes

Costumes

Dancer _____

Dance	Costume	Accessories	Shoes

Costumes

Dancer _____

Dance	Costume	Accessories	Shoes

Costumes

Dancer _____

Dance	Costume	Accessories	Shoes

Costumes

Dancer _____

Dance	Costume	Accessories	Shoes

the
COMP DANCE
Life

"I never knew I had dance moves... until I became a dance mom and started grooving in the audience."

Visit TheCompDanceLife.com to get our free list of must-have items for the upcoming competition season, packed with unique finds you've never seen before and handy links to make shopping a breeze!

Dance Comp Weekend Packing List Ideas

1. Dance Essentials
- Dance costumes (double-check accessories!)
- Extra tights (always bring backups)
- Dance shoes (ballet, jazz, tap, etc...whatever you need for your dances)
- Hair accessories (hairpieces, hats, etc)
- Makeup (studio-approved colors)
- Makeup remover wipes
- Safety pins and sewing kit (for quick fixes)
- Backup rhinestones or embellishments for last-minute repairs
- steamer
- bandaids
- dance bra
- dance underwear
- earrings
- costume glue or tape
- nail polish remover

2. Hair and Beauty
- Hairbrush and part comb
- Hairspray and gel (extra hold!)
- Hair elastics and bobby pins
- Hairnets for buns
- Curling iron/flat iron
- False eyelashes and glue
- Makeup mirrors with lights
- Baby wipes and tissues
- deodorant

3. Comfort Items
- Dance mom chair (foldable and comfy!)
- Dance Mom stool
- Blankets or cozy hoodie
- Snacks and water bottles (for both dancer and mom!)
- Cooler for perishable snacks
- Phone charger and portable power bank
- Headphones/AirPods for downtime

Comp Packing

Comp Packing

the COMP DANCE Life

"You know you're a dance mom when you start using 'point your toes!' as a regular phrase at home."

Hotel Reservations

Dates	Hotel	Confirmation

the
COMP DANCE
Life

You know you're a dance mom when your car smells like hairspray, sequins are your new best friend, and you can do a perfect bun in 60 seconds flat!

Solo Ideas

Dancer	Song	Genre

Solo Ideas

Dancer	Song	Genre

Solo Ideas

Dancer	Song	Genre

Solo Ideas

THE COMP DANCE LIFE

Dancer	Song	Genre

Solo Ideas

Dancer	Song	Genre

the
COMP DANCE
Life

"Dance mom life: I've mastered the quick-change,
but I still can't find my keys."

Comp Journal

Date	Comp	Dance	Adjudication	Overall	Specialty

Comp Journal

Date	Comp	Dance	Adjudication	Overall	Specialty

Comp Journal

Date	Comp	Dance	Adjudication	Overall	Specialty

Comp Journal

Date	Comp	Dance	Adjudication	Overall	Specialty

Date	Comp	Dance	Adjudication	Overall	Specialty

Comp Journal

Date	Comp	Dance	Adjudication	Overall	Specialty

Comp Journal

Date	Comp	Dance	Adjudication	Overall	Specialty

Comp Journal

Date	Comp	Dance	Adjudication	Overall	Specialty

Comp Journal

Date	Comp	Dance	Adjudication	Overall	Specialty

Date	Comp	Dance	Adjudication	Overall	Specialty

Comp Journal

Date	Comp	Dance	Adjudication	Overall	Specialty

Comp Mom TO DO ♥

- [ ] _____
- [ ] _____
- [ ] _____
- [ ] _____
- [ ] _____
- [ ] _____
- [ ] _____
- [ ] _____
- [ ] _____
- [ ] _____
- [ ] _____
- [ ] _____
- [ ] _____
- [ ] _____
- [ ] _____
- [ ] _____

Comp Mom TO DO ♥

- [ ] _____
- [ ] _____
- [ ] _____
- [ ] _____
- [ ] _____
- [ ] _____
- [ ] _____
- [ ] _____
- [ ] _____
- [ ] _____
- [ ] _____
- [ ] _____
- [ ] _____
- [ ] _____
- [ ] _____
- [ ] _____

Comp Mom TO DO ♥

- [ ] _____
- [ ] _____
- [ ] _____
- [ ] _____
- [ ] _____
- [ ] _____
- [ ] _____
- [ ] _____
- [ ] _____
- [ ] _____
- [ ] _____
- [ ] _____
- [ ] _____
- [ ] _____
- [ ] _____
- [ ] _____

Comp Mom TO DO ♥

- [ ] _____
- [ ] _____
- [ ] _____
- [ ] _____
- [ ] _____
- [ ] _____
- [ ] _____
- [ ] _____
- [ ] _____
- [ ] _____
- [ ] _____
- [ ] _____
- [ ] _____
- [ ] _____
- [ ] _____
- [ ] _____
- [ ] _____

Comp Mom TO DO ♥

- [ ] _____
- [ ] _____
- [ ] _____
- [ ] _____
- [ ] _____
- [ ] _____
- [ ] _____
- [ ] _____
- [ ] _____
- [ ] _____
- [ ] _____
- [ ] _____
- [ ] _____
- [ ] _____
- [ ] _____
- [ ] _____

Comp Mom TO DO ♥

- [ ] _____
- [ ] _____
- [ ] _____
- [ ] _____
- [ ] _____
- [ ] _____
- [ ] _____
- [ ] _____
- [ ] _____
- [ ] _____
- [ ] _____
- [ ] _____
- [ ] _____
- [ ] _____
- [ ] _____
- [ ] _____

Comp Mom TO DO ♥

- [ ] _____
- [ ] _____
- [ ] _____
- [ ] _____
- [ ] _____
- [ ] _____
- [ ] _____
- [ ] _____
- [ ] _____
- [ ] _____
- [ ] _____
- [ ] _____
- [ ] _____
- [ ] _____
- [ ] _____

notes

 notes

notes

notes

notes

 notes

notes

 notes

 notes

 notes

 notes

 notes

notes

notes

 notes

 notes

the
COMP DANCE
Life

"I'm not just a mom—I'm a sequined, hairspray-wielding, costume-carrying, snack-preparing warrior."

'The Dance Mom' Cocktail

Ingredients:
2 oz vodka
4 oz sugar-free club soda
2 oz sugar-free lemonade
4-5 cucumber slices
2-3 jalapeño slices (adjust for desired heat)
Ice
Cucumber slice and jalapeño for garnish (optional)

Instructions:
Muddle Cucumber and Jalapeño:
In a shaker or glass, muddle the cucumber slices and jalapeño slices together to release their flavors. The more you muddle, the spicier the drink will be.
Add Vodka and Lemonade:
Pour in the vodka and sugar-free lemonade. Stir or shake well to combine.
Strain and Pour:
Strain the mixture into a glass filled with ice. Top off with the sugar-free club soda.
Garnish:
Garnish with an additional cucumber slice and a jalapeño slice for a fun and spicy presentation.

Serve:
Serve immediately and enjoy the refreshing kick of this cocktail, perfect for dance moms who need a little pick-me-up after a long day!

This drink is light, refreshing, and has just the right amount of spice to make it interesting—just like the dance mom life!

'The Dance Mom Mimosa'

Ingredients:
- 1 part orange juice
- 1 part champagne or prosecco
- Fresh berries or an orange slice for garnish
-

Instructions:
1. Start by filling your favorite comp weekend cup halfway with champagne or prosecco.
2. Add an equal part of orange juice.
3. Garnish with fresh berries or an orange slice to keep things fancy.

Tip: Make it a "mocktail" by swapping out the champagne for sparkling water or ginger ale for those days you need to stay sharp!

Cheers to all the dance moms making it through long competition weekends with style!

'The Dance Mom Espresso Martini'

For when you neeed caffeine during long comp weekends!

Ingredients:
- 1 shot of store-bought espresso (cold brew espresso works perfectly!)
- 1 shot of vodka
- 1/2 shot of coffee liqueur (like Kahlúa)
- 1/2 shot of simple syrup (or adjust to taste)
- Ice cubes
- Coffee beans for garnish

Instructions:
1. Pour the store-bought espresso into a cocktail shaker.
2. Add the vodka, coffee liqueur, and simple syrup to the shaker.
3. Fill the shaker with ice and shake vigorously for 15-20 seconds to chill.
4. Strain into your favorite comp weekend cup
5. Garnish with coffee beans

Ready to keep you energized and fabulous for all things dance mom!

Visit us at
www.TheCompDanceLife.com

and Coming Soon...

Dance Mom Personal Assistant App

The Comp Dance LIfe Survival Guide and Journal
Published by Golden Crown Publishing, LLC

www.GoldenCrownPublishing.com

Created by Melanie Salas
ISBN:978-1-965569-06-1

Made in the USA
Coppell, TX
25 November 2024

41051544R00063